GETTING TO KNOW
THE U.S. PRESIDENTS

DWIGHT D.
EISENHOWER

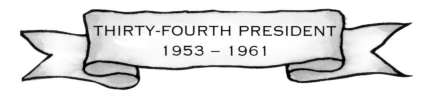

THIRTY-FOURTH PRESIDENT
1953 – 1961

WRITTEN AND ILLUSTRATED BY MIKE VENEZIA

D1376868

CHILDREN'S PRESS
AN IMPRINT OF SCHOLASTIC INC.
NEW YORK   TORONTO   LONDON   AUCKLAND   SYDNEY
MEXICO CITY   NEW DELHI   HONG KONG
DANBURY, CONNECTICUT

PAULINE HAASS PUBLIC LIBRARY

Reading Consultant: Nanci R. Vargus, Ed.D., Assistant Professor, School of Education, University of Indianapolis

Historical Consultant: Marc J. Selverstone, Ph.D., Assistant Professor, Miller Center of Public Affairs, University of Virginia

Photographs © 2007: Art Resource, NY/John Steuart Curry/Smithsonian American Art Museum, Washington, D.C.: 10; Bridgeman Art Library International Ltd., London/New York/Private Collection/Archives Charmet: 6; Corbis Images: 9 top, 25, 28, 32 (Bettmann), 29 (Jerry Cooke), 8, 22 (Hulton-Deutsch Collection); Dwight D. Eisenhower Library: 3, 9 bottom, 13, 14, 15, 17, 18, 20; Library of Congress: 7; Superstock, Inc.: 26.

Colorist for illustrations: Andrew Day

Library of Congress Cataloging-in-Publication Data

Venezia, Mike.
  Dwight D. Eisenhower / written and illustrated by Mike Venezia.
     p. cm. — (Getting to know the U.S. Presidents)
  ISBN-13: 978-0-516-22638-5 (lib. bdg.)   978-0-531-17944-4 (pbk.)
  ISBN-10: 0-516-22638-X (lib. bdg.)   0-531-17944-3 (pbk.)
  1. Eisenhower, Dwight D. (Dwight David), 1890-1969—Juvenile
literature. 2. Presidents—United States—Biography—Juvenile
literature. I. Title. II. Series.

  E836.V46 2007
  973.921092—dc22
  [B]
                                          2006023366

No part of this publication may be reproduced in whole or in part, or stored in a retrieval system, or transmitted in any form or by any means, electronic, mechanical, photocopying, recording, or otherwise, without written permission of the publisher. For information regarding permission, write to Scholastic Inc., 557 Broadway, New York, NY 10012.

Copyright 2007 by Mike Venezia.
All rights reserved. Published in 2007 by Children's Press, an imprint of Scholastic Library Publishing. Published simultaneously in Canada.
Printed in China.

SCHOLASTIC, CHILDREN'S PRESS, and associated logos are trademarks and/or registered trademarks of Scholastic Inc.

1 2 3 4 5 6 7 8 9 10 R 17 16 15 14 13 12 11 10 09 08   62

A portrait of President Dwight D. Eisenhower

Dwight D. Eisenhower was the thirty-fourth president of the United States. He was born in Denison, Texas, on October 14, 1890. Before becoming president, Dwight Eisenhower had been a World War II military hero and one of the most important generals in American history.

During World War II (1939-1945), the United States, England, Canada, and other countries joined together as allies to fight Adolf Hitler's Nazi army in Europe. Allied forces also battled against Japan in the Pacific Ocean. It was the most destructive war ever.

General Eisenhower's job was to win the European part of the war. In 1943, President Franklin Roosevelt named Dwight Eisenhower Supreme Allied Commander. This was a huge promotion that put Eisenhower in charge of all armies fighting Nazi Germany. Roosevelt wanted Eisenhower to head up an Allied invasion that would stop the German army.

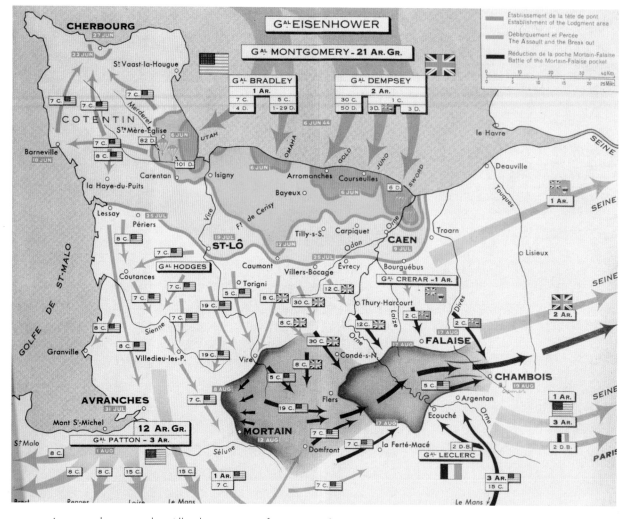

A map showing the Allied invasion of Normandy

The invasion General Eisenhower helped plan was known as Operation Overlord. The exact day of the invasion was called D-Day. During the war, Adolf Hitler's army had taken over or attacked countries in North Africa. He also invaded European countries, including Poland, Belgium, Holland, Russia, and France.

General Eisenhower hoped to surprise the German army on the beaches of Normandy, France. The plan was to drive Hitler's army out of France and back into Germany. This risky invasion was the largest gathering of forces in the history of the world. Thousands of ships, fighter planes, and soldiers gathered off the coast of England. They were ready and waiting to receive General Eisenhower's instructions.

General Eisenhower talks to paratroopers before they parachute into France on D-Day, June 6, 1944.

The U.S. troops that landed in Normandy on D-Day under the command of General Eisenhower were part of an all-out assault on northern France. It was the beginning of a sweep through Europe that would finally defeat Nazi Germany.

On June 6, 1944, General Eisenhower gave his order, "OK, let's go," and the D-Day invasion was on. Thousands of lives were lost, but the Allied armies eventually forced the Nazi army back into Germany.

Knowing he would soon lose the war, Adolf Hitler committed suicide on April 30, 1945. A few days later, Germany surrendered. The war against Japan would rage on for a few more months, but the war in Europe was over! General Eisenhower returned home a hero.

Adolf Hitler

General Eisenhower is welcomed home a hero during a parade in New York City on June 19, 1945.

When Dwight Eisenhower was a baby, his family moved from Denison, Texas, to Abilene, Kansas. Mr. Eisenhower got a job at a dairy there. Dwight had two older brothers and three younger brothers. All of them were called "Ike" at one time or another, but that nickname stuck with Dwight throughout his life. The Eisenhower boys had a happy life growing up in their Kansas farm town.

Dwight Eisenhower grew up on a Kansas farm a lot like the one shown in this John Steuart Curry painting, *The Homestead and the Building of the Barbed Wire Fences.*

Dwight learned important lessons from what went on around him. Once, when he was about four years old, Ike kept getting chased around by a gang of angry geese. The geese kept bullying Ike until he fought back with a broom. Ike learned then that the best way to deal with an enemy was from a position of strength.

Ike was an average student in school,
except when it came to math and sports. Ike
loved playing baseball and football. When he
was in eighth grade, Ike scraped his knee. It
was a small cut, but it soon became infected.
Suddenly, Ike's leg swelled up like a balloon.

Antibiotics hadn't been discovered yet, and Ike was at risk of losing his leg. Doctors wanted to cut it off above the knee to save Ike's life. Dwight Eisenhower refused, though. He said he'd rather die than not be able to play football again. Ike asked his older brother, Edgar, to sleep outside his room and guard against any doctors who might try to sneak in and operate.

Dwight Eisenhower (front center) as a teenager

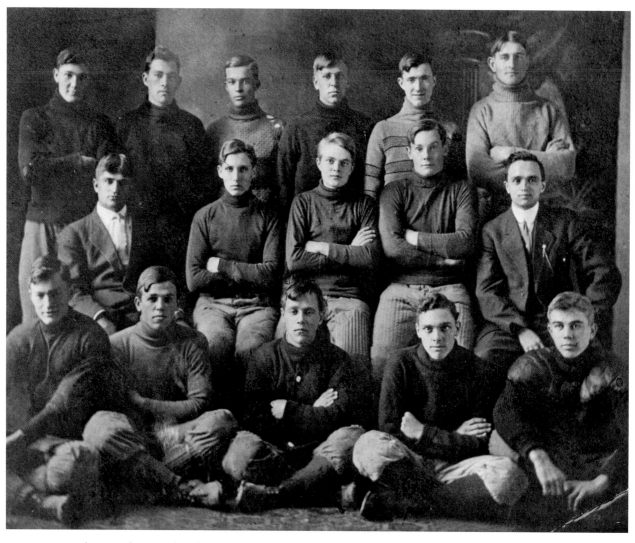

Dwight Eisenhower (back row, third from left) and the members of the Abilene High School football team

Ike could be a stubborn boy. In this case, it paid off. Miraculously, his leg slowly began to get better. Ike went on to become a football star in high school and in college, when he went to the U.S. Military Academy at West Point.

Eisenhower as a West Point cadet in 1911

Ike never had any particular desire to be a soldier. He went to West Point mainly because the education was free if he agreed to serve in the army. The school also had a great football team.

After Ike graduated, in 1915, he was sent around to different army bases to train new soldiers. At an army base in Texas, Ike met the love of his life, Mamie Doud.

Mamie was from a wealthy Colorado family that owned a winter home near the army base. Mamie and Ike fell in love right away. They ended up getting married just a few months later, in 1916.

Dwight Eisenhower and his bride, Mamie, shortly after their wedding in 1916

Even though Mamie wasn't used to the rough military life, she made it her goal to help Ike become the best soldier possible. Over the years, Ike and Mamie moved to dozens of different army bases. They had two sons, Icky and John. Sadly, their first son, Icky, died from scarlet fever when he was only three years old. Ike and Mamie never got over their loss.

During World War I, Eisenhower (left) trained soldiers to use tanks.

During his army career, Ike was lucky to assist some of the best commanding officers in the U.S. military. They included General John Pershing, Douglas MacArthur, and George C. Marshall. These men learned to depend on Ike. They realized he was an exceptionally talented leader. They made sure Ike was sent to special training schools and gave him important jobs.

The United States entered World War I in 1917. Ike's job was training troops to use the latest modern weapon of the time, the motorized tank. Ike was itching to try out the tank in battle, but the war ended before he and his men got the chance.

Ike then volunteered to join an army convoy driving across the country from Washington, D.C., to San Francisco. The army was curious to test U.S. roads in case they were needed in the event of a national emergency.

This photo, from Eisenhower's own collection, was taken during his trip to check the nation's roads. It includes a note in his handwriting, referring to the bridge that the truck is about to cross: "hoping it will hold."

Ike learned many of the nation's roads were in terrible shape, or even unusable! The trip took over two months. Ike never forgot the experience. He knew that someday, someone would have to do something to fix the problem. What Ike didn't know at the time was that he would be the one to do it.

When the United States entered World War II in 1941, Ike was called to Washington, D.C., to help work on war plans. He was then sent to England to set up military operations there. At first, Ike found that British and American soldiers weren't very friendly toward each other. This was a serious problem. The likeable, open-minded Ike went to work right away to fix things.

The Rock of Gibraltar

Ike managed to win the trust and respect of both American and British soldiers. Ike's ability to get people to work together and make things run smoothly helped win important battles in North Africa, Sicily, and Italy. For part of the war, General Eisenhower had a command office in the safety of a cave deep inside the giant Rock of Gibraltar.

When World War II ended, many people tried to get Ike interested in running for president. At first, Ike had no interest at all. Instead, he took a job as head of Columbia University in New York City.

Two years later, President Harry Truman appointed Eisenhower to be supreme commander of the North Atlantic Treaty Organization. NATO was set up to keep the peace between Western European nations and the Soviet Union. During this time, leaders from both the Democratic and Republican parties kept after Ike to run for president.

Dwight D. Eisenhower campaigning
for president in 1952

Finally, in 1952, Ike
agreed to run as the
Republican candidate.
Ike easily won the
election. The slogan
"I Like Ike" caught on
right away.

An automobile bumper
sign supporting Eisenhower
during the 1952
presidential campaign

Eisenhower was president during a time when the U.S. economy was good. Many people had enough money to buy nice homes and fancy new cars.

Dwight D. Eisenhower was president for two four-year terms. It was one of the best times in the United States. There seemed to be plenty of jobs around. Many people were able to buy homes, televisions, and cool-looking cars for the first time. Rock 'n' roll music had just been invented! In 1956, Ike signed a bill to start building modern highways across the country, too.

On the other hand, it was an extremely dangerous time in American history. Just after Ike was elected president, he traveled to the Asian country of South Korea. Communist North Korea had just invaded South Korea. The United States had sent soldiers there to help the South Koreans. Ike wanted to end the fighting. He remembered his childhood lesson with the geese bullies. Ike let it be known that if the war didn't stop, he would be willing to use the United States' new atomic weapons against North Korea. Soon after this, North and South Korea came to an agreement, and the fighting stopped.

The Soviet Army marching through Red Square in Moscow in 1954

Another big worry during the 1950s was dealing with the Soviet Union. The Russians, who were once friendly with the United States, now had their own atomic bomb. They seemed determined to force their way of Communist life on the world. Russian leaders thought people would be better off if the government controlled businesses, railroads, factories, and farms.

Under Communism, people lost many of their rights and freedoms. Anyone who spoke out against it might be sent to prison, or even killed. Ike's biggest challenge was to stop Communism from spreading into free countries without starting a third world war.

President Eisenhower (center) and Vice President Richard Nixon (fourth from left) meeting with Soviet Premier Nikita Khrushchev (third from right) in Washington, D.C., in 1959

President Eisenhower did a great job keeping the United States out of war. This may have been his most important accomplishment. He received criticism, though, for not doing enough to support the rights of African Americans. Ike did sign an important bill that protected African-American voters, but many people felt he could have done more.

Then, in 1960, just when peace talks with the Soviet Union seemed to be going better than ever, something really bad happened.

A U.S. spy plane crashed in the Soviet Union. At first, President Eisenhower denied it was a spy plane, but soon he had to admit he had lied. The Russians were furious! This incident hurt future peace talks for years.

After he retired, former President Eisenhower (shown here with former Vice President Nixon in 1961) spent lots of time relaxing and playing golf.

In 1961, Ike and Mamie left the White House and retired to their farm in Gettysburg, Pennsylvania. Ike spent time painting pictures and playing his favorite game, golf. He wrote a few books and gave advice to other presidents.

Dwight Eisenhower died on March 28, 1969. Even though Ike was one of the greatest military leaders ever, he hated war. Ike worked harder than anyone to keep the world at peace. This was one reason people really did like Ike!

PAULINE HAASS PUBLIC LIBRARY
N64 W23820 MAIN STREET
SUSSEX, WISCONSIN 53089
(262) 246-5180   9/07